SEE A PLANT GROW!

MAPLE TREE

by Charlie W. Sterling

I0801082

TABLE OF CONTENTS

tadpole books

WORDS TO KNOW

branches

buds

leaves

maple tree

seeds

wings

MAPLE TREE

This is a new maple tree.

It grows big.

It takes years.

The leaves change color in fall.

They fall.

Buds grow in spring.

They grow on branches.

Seeds grow.

They grow wings.

They fall.

They spin.

shoot

They grow into new trees!

LET'S REVIEW!

Maple tree seeds are sometimes called helicopters. Can you see why?

INDEX